GUIDE TO
MARTIAL ARTS

GUIDE TO
MARTIAL ARTS

A Step-by-Step Introduction to Taekwondo, Judo, Ju-jitsu, Karate & Kung Fu

JOHN GOLDMAN, 6TH DAN

with special photography by
Charles Parsons

SMITHMARK

In memory of the late Stan Griffiths,
7th Dan Master of the Martial Arts.
He was an inspiration to me on the mat,
a great friend off the mat.

This edition published in 1997 by SMITHMARK Publishers,
a division of U.S. Media Holdings, Inc., 115 West 18th Street,
New York, NY 10011.

SMITHMARK books are available for bulk purchase for sales promotion
and premium use. For details write or call the manager of special sales,
SMITHMARK Publishers, 115 West 18th Street, New York, NY 10011.

This book was designed and produced by
Todtri Productions Limited P.O. Box 572, New York,
NY 10116-0572 FAX: (212) 695-6688

Printed and bound in Singapore

Library of Congress Catalog Card Number 97-066060
ISBN 0-7651-9242-X

Author: John Goldman

Publisher: Robert M. Tod
Designer: Vic Giolitto
Art Director: Ron Pickless
Editor: Nicolas Wright
Typeset and DTP: Blanc Verso/UK

Photo Credits

All photographs by Charles Parsons,
with the exception of the following:

Action-Plus Photographic:
Tony Henshaw—8, 9, 13, 37, 63
Steve Bardens—10, 11 (top), 89
Mike Hewitt—11 (bottom)
Glyn Kirk—117

Sylvio L. Dokov: 24

CONTENTS

INTRODUCTION

WHAT ARE THE MARTIAL ARTS?

Many people still think of the martial arts as a kind of muscular miracle: frail women confront massive, aggressive males and, with a deft turn or two of the wrist, pin them to the ground begging for mercy.

This is not entirely fantasy. Some of the skills you may learn could be used, but only as a last resort, as defence in a real-life situation. But one would have to be very advanced in the martial arts to use them effectively in this way.

FACT OR FICTION?

So where does this leave all those spectacular feats we hear about or see on the films? The hero leaps ten feet in the air, does a back flip and knocks out two villains with a double-splits kick before landing neatly back on his feet. Could this happen?

Well, not so long ago the four-minute mile was an athlete's dream; now it is not all that unusual. In the martial arts a mix of gymnastics and martial techniques produce the spectacular.

Can a Taekwondo expert leap ten feet in the air and kick through a thick wooden board? It has been done. Can one man take on ten attackers at once and beat them? This is no more incredible than other feats on the record.

There is a story about a Karate master who selected a tree in a nearby forest and, returning each day, kicked and punched the trunk thousands of times. The tree died but he ended up with hands and feet so hard that a blow from him was like being felled by an iron bar. Another master worked up so much power that when he punched the ground his arm went into the earth up to his elbow.

HOW COMPETITIVE?

Martial arts today are taught as pure skills or as sport. Pupils receive instruction under strict supervision. In some of these arts, like Judo—an Olympic sport—contact is made in attack and defence but under careful control, always with safety in mind. Martial arts contests are no different from other competition, with athletes going all out for their teams and spectators cheering them on.

WHEN DID IT ALL START?

Today's martial arts have developed from warring techniques, with or without the use of weapons. They were battlefield skills devised for killing or maiming an adversary.

Combat skills of some form have been practised as far back—well, your guess is as good as mine. The first records of unarmed fighting skills are engravings and murals found in Egyptian pyramids dating back 5,000 years.

For more organised systems of combat skills we look to the ancient Greeks. They developed wrestling techniques which, coupled with boxing, became a popular sport introduced into the Olympic games in 648 B.C. These contests were brutal, often resulting in serious injury or even death.

Most of the martial arts we practise today developed from the fighting skills of the Far East. They spread through Asia and China to Japan.

Travelling monks and priests were often attacked by robbers and equipped themselves with defence skills. Peasants learned to fight in order to defend their livestock, crops, homes and families against marauding bandits. They used punching and kicking techniques but they also became skilled in the use of their farming implements as weapons.

The *tonfa*, an oak rod for pounding soya, and the *sai*, a short swordlike implement dragged through the soil to make a trough for planting seeds, became lethal weapons. Today martial arts exponents still use modified forms of these farming implements.

WHICH IS BEST—
HOW DO I CHOOSE?

There's a vast range of martial arts for you to choose from. Some rely on the use of bare hands and feet, others include weaponry. Some individual arts have many styles: there are more than seventy different forms of Karate and literally hundreds of different kinds of Chinese Kung Fu.

Then there is Kendo—the way of the sword—developed from the Japanese Samurai skills of swordsmanship. Also from Japan comes Aikido, a defensive art of locking joints and throwing evolved from ancient Ju-Jitsu techniques intended to incapacitate or kill an opponent.

The best martial art for you is the one you enjoy most. People are attracted for different reasons.

The Author and His Family

Martial arts run through the Goldman family like a special gene. The youngest member, Alex, was tumbling around the mat as soon as he could toddle and is now a keen and quite talented learner. His aunt Jenny looks admiringly at him, remembering the time when she herself stole a television show—almost before she could walk—by crawling, uninvited, on to the mat and diverting the attention of the cameras to herself. Ruth, on the right, is a Black belt and, like her father John (in the front with Alex), a professional instructor. John's wife, Chris, at the centre back, is perfectly at home with her fighting family, for she is also a Black belt. She partners 6th Dan Black belt John in his many martial arts activities, including the running of classes, clubs and rallies.

Overleaf: The opening ceremony at the 1988 Seoul Olympics.

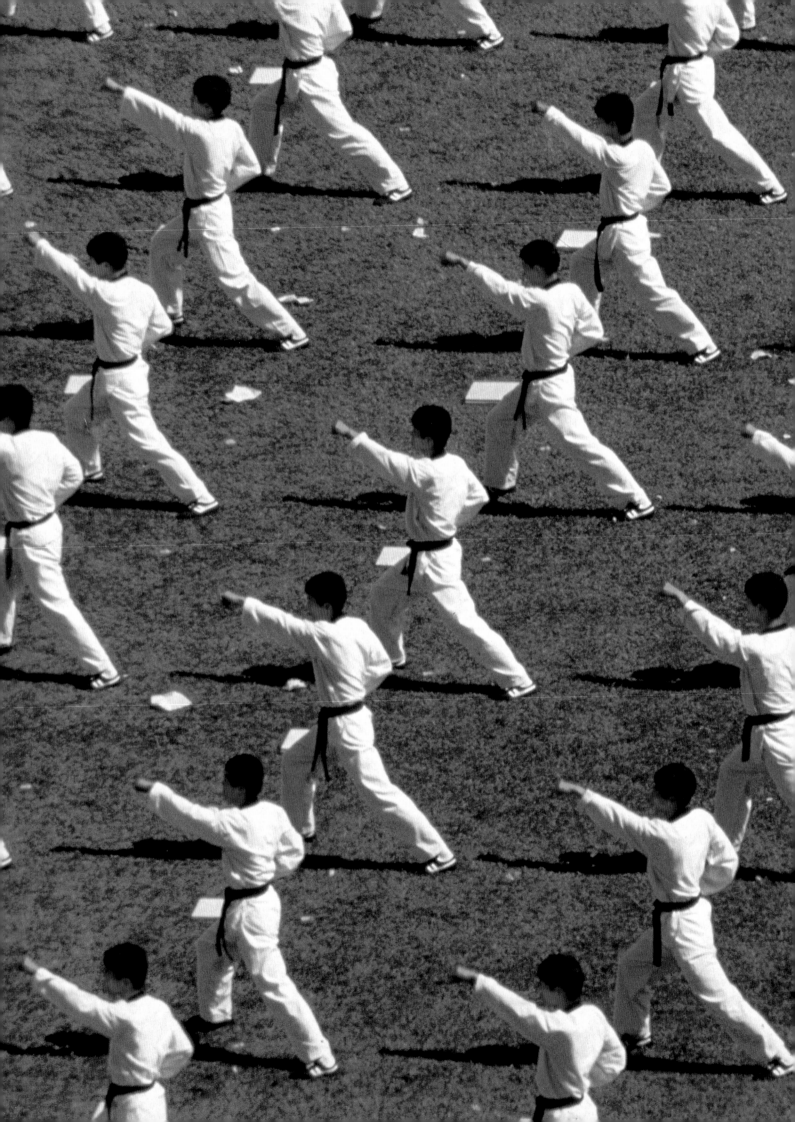

There are those who just want to have a go. Some want to get or keep fit. Many regard it as a sort of self-defence. You'll soon find there's a lot more to the martial arts than you thought. Training will bring benefits beyond your expectations whether you choose to be competitive or non-competitive.

In some styles the learning and perfecting of techniques are pursuits of their own with competition a secondary consideration. In any case the martial arts are not just physical—they are mentally stimulating and they promote self-development. And of course you'll make new friends, gain personal confidence and have lots of fun.

AM I TOO YOUNG, TOO OLD?

There are millions of martial arts practitioners world-wide and of all ages. I know a man in his seventies who can still make a neat throw on a good day. My five-year-old grandson Alex beams with excitement when he knows it's time for his Judo lessons.

The arts are safe for everyone if you follow the rules. Each training hall (*dojo*) will have a set of rules. Safety, courtesy and respect for each other are as much a part of the martial arts as the learning of techniques.

The martial arts have something to offer everyone. People with disabilities take part. I know blind people who do Judo and a man with one arm who is a Karate Black Belt. People in wheelchairs also practise the martial arts, adapting techniques to suit their needs. That's the beauty of the martial arts. Skills can be developed, honed and modified, ensuring a lifetime of pleasure. Once you get started you're hooked for life.

HOW DO I GET STARTED?

This book is not intended as an in-depth study of the martial arts. It is a guide to a part of a vast range of techniques practised world-wide. I hope it will encourage you and help you decide which art to choose.

IN THE INTERESTS OF SAFETY, DO NOT PRACTISE ANY MARTIAL ARTS MOVES, INCLUDING THOSE IN THIS BOOK, WITHOUT THE SUPERVISION OF A QUALIFIED COACH.

Once you join a club and get started, you'll be able to use this book as reference to some of the techniques you'll be learning.

Go along to your local club for a chat with the instructor. The atmosphere there should be friendly. The going may look tough but there should be no injuries. You should be able to join in a few sessions to see if it's right for you. Then you'll need to buy a uniform; usually the club holds a stock.

After a few months it will be time to enter your first grading examination. This should earn you your first belt or sash.

Remember, we all progress at different speeds; there is no race to the top. As one great master and philosopher said 'There are no short cuts because there is no end.'

The idea is to enjoy yourself and discover all the benefits to be gained by taking part. Good luck!

Part 1
TAEKWONDO

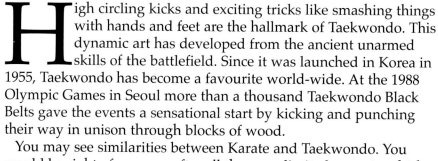igh circling kicks and exciting tricks like smashing things with hands and feet are the hallmark of Taekwondo. This dynamic art has developed from the ancient unarmed skills of the battlefield. Since it was launched in Korea in 1955, Taekwondo has become a favourite world-wide. At the 1988 Olympic Games in Seoul more than a thousand Taekwondo Black Belts gave the events a sensational start by kicking and punching their way in unison through blocks of wood.

You may see similarities between Karate and Taekwondo. You would be right of course—after all there are limited ways in which you can use hands and feet as weapons. All the same you will see from the following pages that the jumping and high circling kicks of Taekwondo are distinctly different from those in Karate. The kicks and strikes performed by the Taekwondoist in prearranged sequences, known as patterns, also differ significantly from the sequences practised in Karate.

Taekwondo players specialise in destruction techniques—the breaking of blocks of wood, ice blocks and tiles, all with their bare hands and feet. The smashing of things is a means of measuring the effectiveness of skills they have learned—it will be a good while before you get involved in these particular activities. It should be encouraging for you to know that the application of science coupled to intense training can produce these astonishing results—without causing any personal damage.

Before we take a look at some of the techniques and training methods of Taekwondo, we should take note of a few important points:

NEVER ATTEMPT ANY DESTRUCTION TECHNIQUES WITHOUT THE SUPERVISION OF A QUALIFIED INSTRUCTOR.

NEVER ALLOW CHILDREN TO TAKE PART IN THESE DESTRUCTION TECHNIQUES, WHICH CAN DAMAGE GROWING BONES AND TISSUES.

AS IN ALL THE MARTIAL ARTS, THE RULES OF SAFETY OVERRIDE ALL ELSE.

WARMING UP, SHAPING UP

Before starting any physical activity the body needs warming up in preparation for the demands of training. Whichever sport you take part in there is always a warming up period.

You begin gently with exercises to mobilise the joints. Then, gradually, you raise the pulse rate. The cardiovascular system, the heart, lungs and circulatory system must be prepared for action. This can be done with simple exercises: walking on the spot, jogging or skipping. However, you'll

find each activity has its own specialised exercises. Flexibility, by way of stretching exercises, is vital to the Taekwondoist, just as a weight training programme produces results for the body builder.

Above: We've only just started and it's time to rest? Not really. Despite my model Vagn's obvious flexibility he always loosens up with an exercise routine and a good stretch.

Left: Christopher (on the floor) will be able to do the chair splits like Vagn within three months.

STANDING STEADY

Good posture and stance are fundamental to all martial arts practice. Some stances appear deceptively passive others look fearsomely strong. However they look, they're not rigid. A stance is like a platform, a launch pad from which you dart to avoid attack or strike out. Some stances are 'on guard' in readiness for attack, others are clearly for action—fighting stances.

Left: This rear foot stance is Shelly's favourite. To her unsuspecting opponent she appears to retreat. Suddenly her front leg will snap out high at the target—her opponent's head. Point!

ON THE MOVE

It's not enough just to learn a series of stances. You need to be able to move from one stance to another—smoothly. Patterns of movements, Tuls and Taegueks, will help you here. At first these patterns may look like an odd assortment of moves. Each pattern may take many lessons to learn but through repetition you'll soon get the idea. You'll move from one stance to another, often at varying speeds, and in different directions. It's a mental discipline as much as a physical one. Often the whole class will practise a pattern together. Drilled in rows you'll be placed at the back, to begin with that is, a sort of follow-my-leader system.

Above and left: This class, all Black belts, move meaningfully from one stance to another. They're halfway through a pattern of nearly forty moves. Some have over seventy! The patterns are designed so that the last move made brings the practitioners back to the exact spot at which they started.

TARGET PRACTICE 1

Timing, accuracy, speed and power divide the winners and losers in any combat sport. There are two formats of Taekwondo competition, semi-contact and full contact. Whichever one you take part in you want to be on target.

We'll talk about the rules in a later chapter. For now, we concentrate on training in readiness for the big test—the competition.

We begin with hand strikes. Here, as a training aid, we use target mitts or focus pads. They are a sort of hand-held glove covered by a firm but flexible pad. Your partner holds the pads at a height and angle at which you can hit them with a selected technique. As you progress, your partner without warning moves the position of the pads. You spring from one position to another, punching and striking. This really does test your reflexes and helps increase your accuracy.

Martin Hopper and Jo are father and daughter. After a flurry of strikes and blows at the pads, Martin thought Jo needed a rest. Wrong. When Martin lowered the pads to finish, Jo took this as a signal to attack. The impact shook Martin.

TARGET PRACTICE 2

Just as the small target mitts are used for developing the speed and accuracy of hand strikes they are also used for focusing and improving kicks. Kicking techniques generally come into play when your opponent is out of reach and you cannot punch or strike.

Philip is Martin's son-in-law. When Philip concentrates on developing more power to his kicks, Martin makes sure he has a heavy duty pad!

TARGET PRACTICE 3

Jumping kicks are undoubtedly the most difficult to develop and the most spectacular to watch. It is here that continual commitment to mobility and flexibility exercises pays dividends.

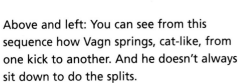

Above and left: You can see from this sequence how Vagn springs, cat-like, from one kick to another. And he doesn't always sit down to do the splits.

ONE STEP SPARRING

Your aim in competition is of course to get the upper hand. In a real life attack your first objective is to get away to safety. You need to know how to avoid whatever an attacker may throw at you. A boxer's training involves practice ducking and weaving to avoid blows. He'll shadow box with an imaginary opponent.

In Taekwondo rigorous attention is paid to the development of evasion and blocking techniques. After all, Taekwondo was designed as an art of defence.

If you can't move out of the way of an attack, because you're not quick enough or you haven't the room, you have to have the ability to block and counter an attack.

The initial blocking action can be done in a variety of ways using hands, arms, knees, legs or feet.

Let's first look at using the hand and arm as a blocking device.

Shelly, left, squares up to Jo. For this prearranged practice Shelly is the attacker. Both these girls are Black belts and have won international titles in their sport. Jo came under real attack one evening. She struck out at her assailant with such force and accuracy that she was able to escape. Although she did not stay around to see the result of her counter-attack she is confident her would-be assailant was left with a sore jaw. That's her first target in the following series of hand blocks and counter strikes.

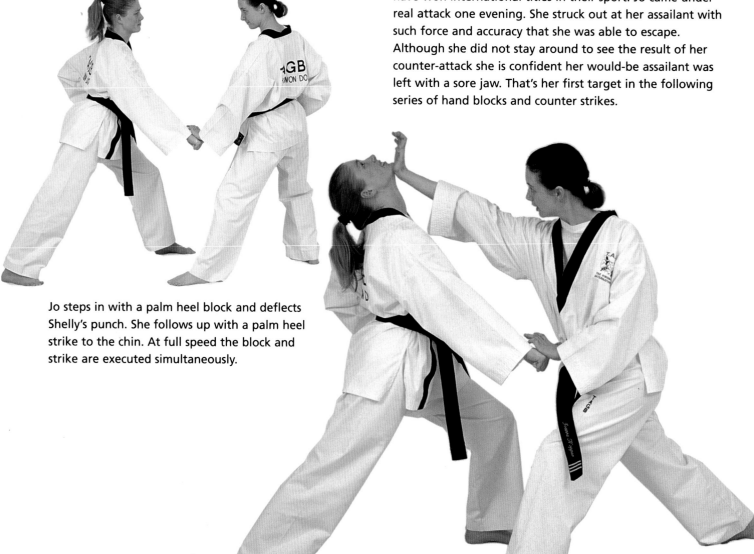

Jo steps in with a palm heel block and deflects Shelly's punch. She follows up with a palm heel strike to the chin. At full speed the block and strike are executed simultaneously.

Good posture and stance are essential in both attack and in defence. Having made a forearm block Jo makes sure that Shelly hasn't got any other ideas up her sleeve. She grabs Shelly's wrist, pulling her off balance. Following up swiftly with a reverse knifehand strike she puts a final stop to her attacker's plans.

Using both arms in a low cross block, Jo positions herself perfectly for a double tops score!

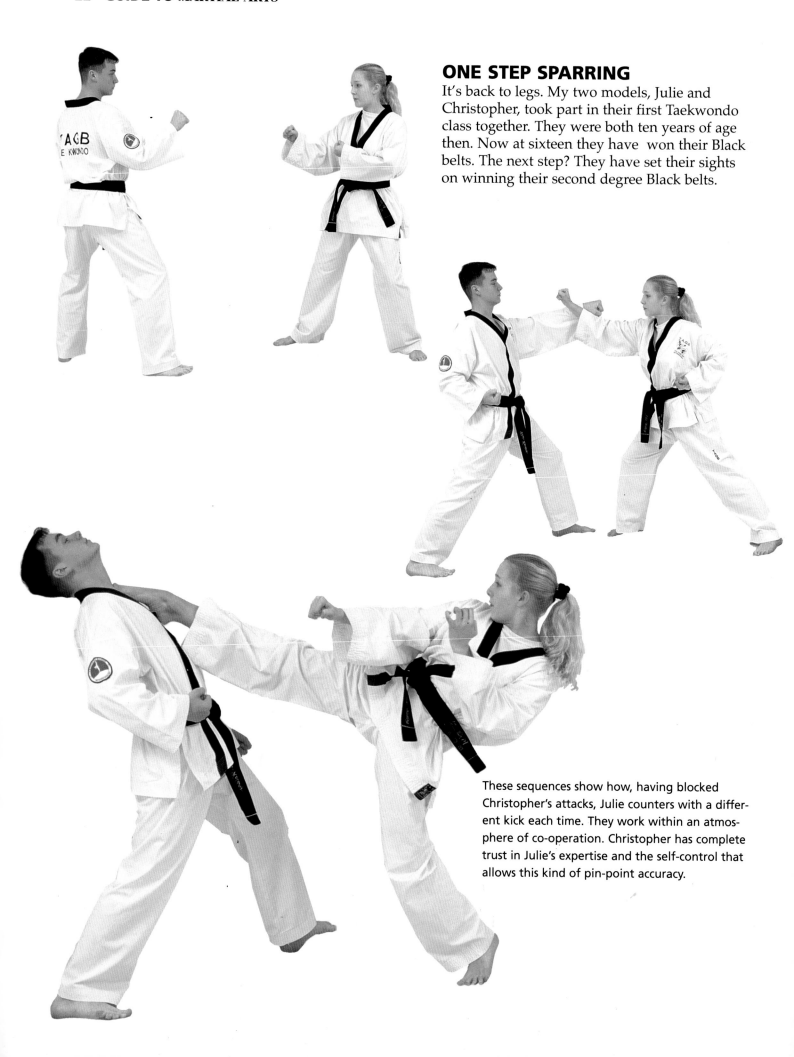

ONE STEP SPARRING

It's back to legs. My two models, Julie and Christopher, took part in their first Taekwondo class together. They were both ten years of age then. Now at sixteen they have won their Black belts. The next step? They have set their sights on winning their second degree Black belts.

These sequences show how, having blocked Christopher's attacks, Julie counters with a different kick each time. They work within an atmosphere of co-operation. Christopher has complete trust in Julie's expertise and the self-control that allows this kind of pin-point accuracy.

Feet, used like hands, are unexpected weapons. There are many areas of the foot you can use to strike with—the ball of the foot, the side of the foot, the instep, the base of the heel, the back of the heel.

PUT TO THE TEST

Although a recognised show-piece, the smashing of tiles, bricks, slabs and wooden boards with bare hands and feet has a deeper meaning to the Taekwondo practitioner.

Feats of destruction are not merely ways to show off. They are a means of testing the accuracy, speed and power of techniques learned in class.

Points to note: children never take part in destruction techniques. Adults only attempt breaking techniques after considerable training and then only under strict supervision. And it's not just a question of smashing.

Quite apart from the physical training, including the use of hand mitts and kick bags to develop a strike and focus on its target, the correct mental approach for attempting any destruction technique is crucial. A sense of complete confidence and concentration is vital. And there is the scientific factor; how the object to be broken is placed or held. Every object breaks once the limit of its resilience has been passed, and you need to know how best to break through this resistance.

Most breaking techniques that you will perform could be described as 'token' breaks. Smashing cleanly, and without personal injury, through a one-inch-thick wooden board demonstrates the practitioner's precision and skill. It also demonstrates the effectiveness of the blow; after all Taekwondo is a martial art.

Right: A world record smash! Token breaks are part and parcel of training. A power break is something different. World record holder Brian Towndrow smashed his way through two piles of concrete kerb stones. Each pile was made up of twenty-one blocks of stones each two inches thick! First a strike with his right elbow crumpled one stack, a blow with his left elbow smashed through a second separate stack. Since that feat Brian has smashed through a mountain of two-inch-thick concrete slabs twenty-two high!

Concentration and focus ensure success for Shelly's and Jo's token breaks. Both Shelly's palm heel strike and Jo's side piercing kick cut clean through two-inch-thick boards.

FIVE-STEP SPARRING

Stances, kicks, strikes and blocks; it's time to put them all together. To begin with you and your partner work through a series of prearranged moves. It's a fight, but each of you knows who is going to attack, and how the other will respond.

You begin with a one-step routine, attack and counter. Then, prearranged sparring will involve moving either three or five steps.

Sparring begins with the attacker in fighting stance. The aggressor steps forward and attacks at a measured speed. This enables the defender to counter each technique one at a time.

After defending against Philip's onslaught of punches with knife hand blocks, Christopher slips, on guard, out of danger and into position for retaliation. All these moves have been performed step by step. In free sparring, or faced with real danger, Christopher's side piercing kick and knife hand strike counter-attack would find their mark like forked lightening.

Julie is used to training with male and female partners and is a formidable opponent to both when it comes to free sparring. However, in this pre-arranged sequence, it's Vagn's turn to come out on top. He twists in with a turning kick.

ON YOUR OWN

One of the most valuable training aids and avenues to perfection in the practice of martial arts is through the practice of patterns. In Judo and Karate they are known as Kata, in Kung Fu as forms.

Each Taekwondo pattern is practised as a solo exercise; a series of defending and attacking movements against imaginary opponents. Patterns are designed to develop and refine technique and hone the student's instincts of awareness. There are many patterns to learn and, as you progress, they become more complex. Each move has a purpose. For each technique there is a real life application.

Many of the techniques can be practised safely in the club or in competition. However, some of the moves, ancient combat skills, are too dangerous to practise with a partner. Performing a pattern allows the student to execute these moves, with full force, on an imaginary opponent.

From a designated starting point the moves of a pattern are performed at differing speeds and in different directions. The final action will bring you back to the exact point at which you started.

As Jo swings in to this final strike she is in full control. Her actions, perfectly balanced both physically and mentally, are razor sharp.

Take a close look. Jo's breathing, co-ordinated with every movement she has made, helps her to focus on her target with precision and power.

DEFENCE—A LAST RESORT

Many people join a martial arts club to learn some form of self-defence. It is true that becoming proficient in a martial art could give you the means for escaping from real danger. However, any form of physical defence learnt in a martial arts club is only to be used as a last resort.

The fact that you have joined a class is a step towards increasing your self-confidence and heightening your powers of awareness.

Most people continue training because they enjoy it. Their original desire to equip themselves with self-defence skills takes on a different guise—deep and lasting interest.

The ancient warrior, even wearing armour, was open to attack. The weak spots, where one piece of armour joined another, would become a target for a well aimed blow. Get-in-close and joint locking techniques could be applied. On the battlefield it was a matter of life or death. In the training hall it is, of course, different!

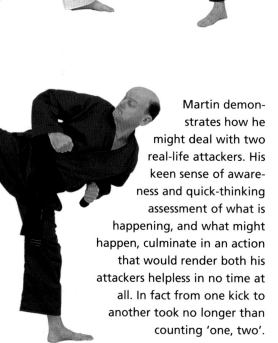

Martin demonstrates how he might deal with two real-life attackers. His keen sense of awareness and quick-thinking assessment of what is happening, and what might happen, culminate in an action that would render both his attackers helpless in no time at all. In fact from one kick to another took no longer than counting 'one, two'.

HIGH FLYERS

Away from the battlefield it's back to practising and perfecting skills for use in the club. Self-achievement and enjoyment is really what Taekwondo is all about. Proceedings of the class will be varied, new skills for you to try your hand at will be introduced constantly.

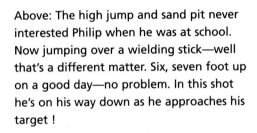

Above: The high jump and sand pit never interested Philip when he was at school. Now jumping over a wielding stick—well that's a different matter. Six, seven foot up on a good day—no problem. In this shot he's on his way down as he approaches his target !

Below: Middle-aged? What's that got to do with it? Martin trains every day. He works out at home before going off to teach at one of his schools. Martin has trained dozens of pupils up to Black belt. Now, apart from giving them ongoing guidance and instruction, he also, from time to time, visits and teaches their students.

FREE SPARRING

The high-jumping kicking skills of Taekwondo are dynamic and spectacular to watch. It is this visual attraction that more often than not catches people's attention and inspires them to try their hand at this fascinating sport.

Likewise, the competitive opportunities of Taekwondo offer encouragement to many would-be champions. There are two forms of competition, semi-contact and full contact. Competitors, padded out in body armour and head protectors, fight in weight groups. Men and women compete separately. The idea is to score points by attacking specific target areas on the opponent's body. At the end of three three-minute bouts the person with the most points is declared the winner.

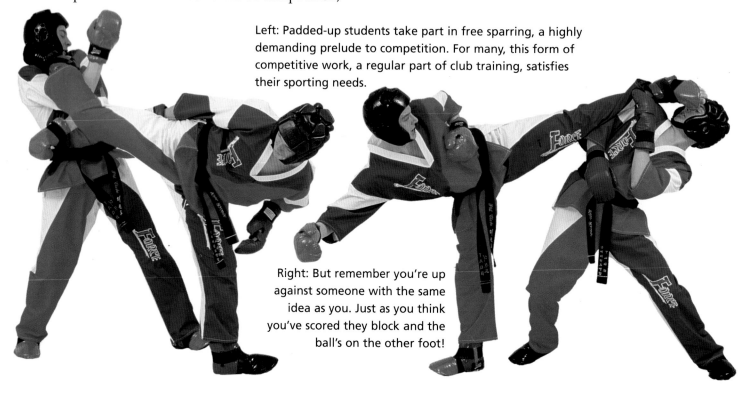

Left: Padded-up students take part in free sparring, a highly demanding prelude to competition. For many, this form of competitive work, a regular part of club training, satisfies their sporting needs.

Right: But remember you're up against someone with the same idea as you. Just as you think you've scored they block and the ball's on the other foot!

Below left and right: It's no different when women Taekwondoists step into action. Jo and Shelly have been training partners for years and are evenly matched.

You'll find that you will favour a few selected techniques. Continual practice of your chosen favourites will bring startling results. Vagn often practises his side piercing kick leaping over a row of four or five of his classmates. They trust him— crouched over to protect their heads, of course.

However, just like my models you'll no doubt want to test your skills out in the safety of free sparring. Do they work? Judge for yourself. I think you'll agree that Julie's do!

Part 2
JUDO

Judo is a combat sport but it's not all fight. There's skill, graceful movement, some cunning and lots of fun. Judo started with a Tokyo schoolmaster called Jigaro Kano. He wanted for his students physical activity that would challenge their minds and teach them self-discipline, courtesy and respect for others. Kano made a study of Ju-Jitsu which, as practised at the time, had its dangers. He discarded certain moves and adapted others in the interests of safety. After years of hard work he launched what was virtually a new sport. Judo, as he called it, was born in 1882.

Judo spread from the schools and universities of Japan to America and the rest of the West. By 1964 it was so universally recognised that it was included in the Tokyo Olympics. Today over ten million people practise Judo world-wide.

There's almost certainly a Judo club near enough for you to join. See the instructor and watch what goes on. It may look tough but notice: is everybody enjoying it without getting hurt? That's how it should be, that's how it must be.

Judo is a sport you'll get hooked on—for life. You begin by learning the art of breakfalling, how to fall without hurting yourself. Then on to some basic throws and holds. Bit by bit the moves will become more complex and more adventurous. Counter and combination techniques, to outwit your opponent, are part of the syllabus. Arm-locking techniques and strangulation holds will follow. Although these moves are all part and parcel of the sport, they are applied within a framework of rules designed for your safety.

As with many other martial arts, Judo has its own katas for you to work. Kata is an in-depth study of Judo techniques, and although physically demanding, is practised in a non-competitive environment. Unlike Karate and Taekwondo, where kata is a solo exercise, you practise the katas of Judo with a partner.

As you progress you will not only develop fresh skills all the time, you'll make your own discoveries. Many new moves thought up by students have become a recognised part of the sport.There are belts to win in recognition of your advancing prowess and you'll read more about this in the pages to follow.

JUDO FOR ALL

People of all ages and abilities take part in Judo. Some have their sights set on becoming Olympic champions. Others want to learn defence. For most, it's a recreational hobby. Practitioners come from all walks of life. Theodore Roosevelt, former president of the United States of America, practised Judo. At the White House he had a room specially prepared for Judo practice.

Education authorities recognise the benefits Judo brings to young people. Many countries include Judo in the schools' national curriculum. That's not surprising—Judo was started by a schoolmaster.

In 1994 two British Judo experts, Brian Woodward and David Norman, set out to see how many throws they could complete in a ten-hour stint. They did a staggering 33,681!

Right: Five-year-old Alex is my grandson. On entering the practice hall (*dojo*) he gives a customary bow. This is the signal that he's ready to take part in the class. The *dojo* is matted out. The padded surface is specially made to reduce some of the impact when you are thrown. Nevertheless you need to fall correctly. Learning how to fall and breakfalling are among the first things you must master. Black belt experts continue to practise breakfalling as part of their warm-up and preparation routine.

Left: Breakfalling: The shock of a fall is reduced by slapping the mat with the palm of your hand and the underside of a straight but relaxed arm. This action is applied with one or two arms, depending on how you are thrown, just before your body hits the mat.

Left: Eleven-year-old Luke has been enjoying Judo for the past four years. He's really into the swing of it as he demonstrates a side breakfall.

Above and bottom left: Note that as Luke falls he looks towards the place of impact—this helps ensure a safe landing.

Another way—as you fall forward, roll, slap the mat and rise again.

HIP THROWS

The practice of any sport has potential dangers. Judo entails throws, holds, armlocks and strangulation techniques. This does not mean taking people to the point of death.

Throws are the most spectacular techniques in Judo. Most people could, with strength and a little knowledge, clumsily attempt to trip someone over. However, there's more to Judo than that. You need total control of your actions.

The idea is to throw your opponent onto their back with speed, impetus and control. Fully succeed in this and you win—*Ippon*. A lesser throw wins you a lesser score. These are just some of the rules. Break the rules and you receive penalty points, or at its worst, disqualification.

You throw your opponent forwards, backwards or to the side. You do this standing or, having sacrificed your own position, lying down. Techniques are classified as hip, hand or leg throws—depending on the throwing action. We begin with a hip throw. My two models, Steve and Chris, demonstrate.

Above: Steve, on the left, sees the way clear to step in for his attack.

Left and right: Steve wraps his arm around Chris, pulling him forward. At the same time he thrusts his hips sideways, in front of and across Chris's hips, in readiness to wheel him over. This technique is called the hip wheel (*Koshi guruma*).

Clockwise: The sleeve lift, pull, hip throw (*Sode tsurikomi goshi*) is an ideal technique for the competitor who likes to grab with both hands at his opponent's sleeves. Note how Steve sinks low under his opponent. 'Getting under the opponent's centre of gravity' is one of the secrets of a successful hip throw.

LEG THROWS

To make a good throw takes commitment. You put your whole body into the action. The two hip throws we have looked at were selected from a vast range of techniques. Apart from the essential use of the hips, they both involved good use of the hands, for pulling and lifting, and the legs for bending and pivoting.

We now look at leg and foot throws. The throwing action of the leg works in co-ordination with hips and hands.

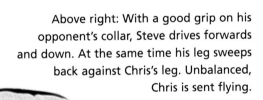

Above: Steve steams towards Chris, his leg poised for action. This leg technique, major outer reaping (*O soto gari*), sweeps the opponent backwards and down to the mat.

Above right: With a good grip on his opponent's collar, Steve drives forwards and down. At the same time his leg sweeps back against Chris's leg. Unbalanced, Chris is sent flying.

Right: Note how Chris instinctively has his arm ready to slap the mat—the all important breakfall!

Clockwise: It's full power ahead. Steve sweeps up inside his opponent's legs. The action is aptly named Inner Thigh throw (*Uchi mata*). It is one of the few leg techniques that throws the opponent forward and is a favourite with competitors of all weight categories.

Uchi mata demonstrates the beauty of a Judo throw. The extended leg and overall body action of the thrower is likened to the poise and grace of a gymnast or dancer.

Clockwise: Another leg throw. The major inner reaping (*O uchi gari*) takes the opponent crashing backwards to the floor. You make sure of this by following in the same direction!

Clockwise and opposite top:
Not a beginner's technique!
To execute this move takes a lot of
experience, total commitment,
and some daring. Leave it, for now
anyway,to our experts Chris and Steve.

Left: This looks like a tangled mess but Steve has kept a grip on Chris. His next move will be to hold Chris down. We will deal with holds and other ground-work techniques shortly.

. . .coming down! Note how Ruth maintains her posture.

Above: Finally, in this selection of leg throws, my daughter Ruth takes up the action. She started Judo at the age of six. Now, twenty-five years on she has attained the rank of Black belt 4th Dan. She demon-strates one of her favourite techniques—how about this foot sweep? With pin-point accuracy, and timing, she catches Chris as he steps sideways. He's hardly on his way up before . . .

HAND THROWS

Once you seize the opportunity to attack you move without delay. A throw, from start to finish, takes just a couple of seconds. Speed of entry for attack and a correct position for throwing are crucial. Part of training time is given to the development of 'winding-in' for an attack (*Uchikomi*). With a co-operative partner you whip in, positioning yourself for a throw, and whip out. You repeat this exercise, in, out, in, out, building up speed.

It's full steam ahead as Ruth takes the helm. She demonstrates, on Chris, two distinctly different hand throws.

Left and right: This shoulder throw (*Morote seoinage*) is a favourite hand technique with competitors. Ruth makes good use of both her hands, lifting and pulling her opponent forward. Note that although Ruth has turned in deeply, her hips and lower back have not made contact.

Below left and right: Now, after the powerful impetus of her hand movements, Ruth makes full body contact. Her opponent has no say in the matter as he is steered towards the mat.

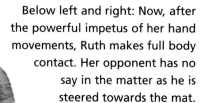

Left: Getting to grips is all part of the game. Different grips suit different players. Ruth snatches her opponent's jacket to effect the hold she wants.

Bottom left and below: Both hands on, Ruth attacks. This throw, the body drop (*Tai otoshi*), is exactly that. Ruth drops beneath her opponent. Driving hands complete the action—it's all over for Chris.

SACRIFICIAL THROWS

We have dealt with hip, hand and leg techniques—now for 'sacrificial' throws. The thrower, maintaining a grip on the opponent's jacket, purposefully falls to the floor. The opponent, unbalanced and toppling, is quickly flipped over. Sacrificial moves need a lot of rehearsing. If they don't succeed, the throwers may find themselves in a weak position—on the floor with the opponent in charge!

Above: From this crouched position Ruth sees a clear space ahead.

Centre left and right: She slips underneath to make a high circle throw (*Tomenage*). Note: both Ruth's legs come into action. Her right is poised to lift and tip Chris over. Her left is ready to assist the 'launch'.

Bottom left: This throw requires full commitment, an explosion of movement and energy. Ruth in full flight follows her actions through.

Bottom right: The throw is completed—Ruth comes out on top!

Top left, right, centre and bottom: The side separation throw (*Yoko wakare*), is ideal to attempt when your opponent is crouched over. Ruth makes strong contact with her opponent's upper body before 'disappearing' underneath. As Chris is hurled over, she rotates her body to follow him. She hasn't finished with him yet; before she's through she'll secure him in a firm hold.

COMBINATION THROWS

It's time to look at combination moves. These are double-action attacks. If one technique doesn't work you immediately switch to another. Competitors begin training with movements that feels natural to them. Having mastered two or three 'speciality' techniques they think ahead. What if the throw doesn't work? What if the opponent makes a defensive move or dives out the way of the attack? All possibilities must be considered. Any action must be directed to make sure the opponent is thrown.

Clockwise: Steve (left) demonstrates a combination technique. He moves in to throw his opponent backwards to the mat. His left foot clips behind Chris's foot. He attempts to sweep Chris's leg away. His opponent is having none of this and stands fast. Steve doesn't hesitate. He switches, hooking his opponent's other leg. Chris wasn't ready—it all happened too quickly. He's going over backwards, whether he likes it or not.

Left: This combination move shows Steve finally throwing his opponent forward. But first, his attempt to throw Chris backwards, with a leg throw, is thwarted.

Right: A change of plan and direction: maintaining his grip, Steve hops around, on one leg, to face the same way as Chris.

Above left and right: Now, with solid body contact and Chris unbalanced, Steve can't fail. Chris is swept off his feet.

COUNTER-ATTACKS

Learning to defend against an attack is, of course, a vital part of training. However, we have seen from the previous demonstrations how the attacker, having met resistance, combines several forms of attack until the opponent is floored. So defending against an attack doesn't always get you out of trouble.

You need a plan. A complete switch around, a counter-attack. It's not merely a question of blocking and stopping an attack and then making a counter throw. You defend, yes. But you cleverly make use of the opponent's attacking movement and 'throw it back' against them.

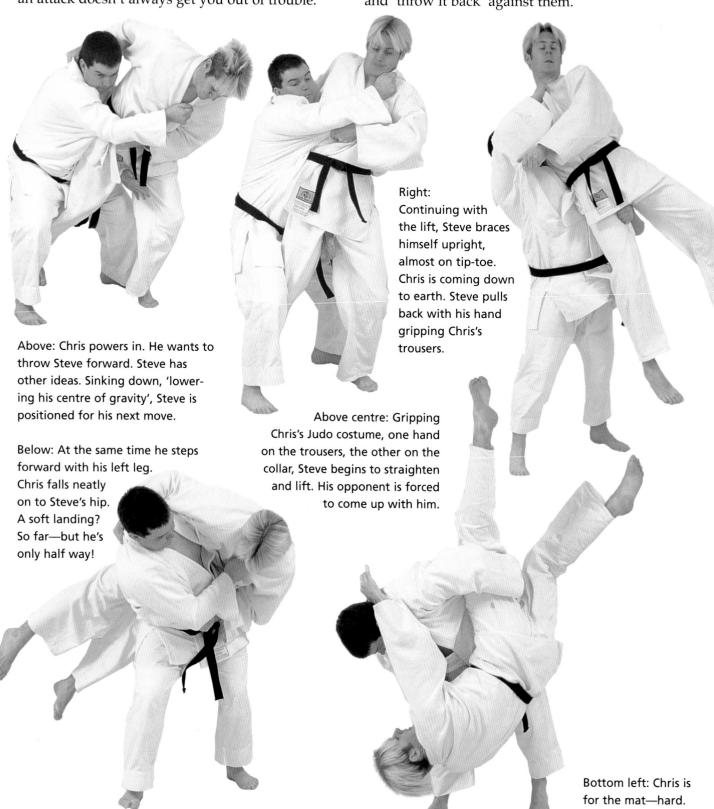

Right:
Continuing with the lift, Steve braces himself upright, almost on tip-toe. Chris is coming down to earth. Steve pulls back with his hand gripping Chris's trousers.

Above: Chris powers in. He wants to throw Steve forward. Steve has other ideas. Sinking down, 'lowering his centre of gravity', Steve is positioned for his next move.

Below: At the same time he steps forward with his left leg. Chris falls neatly on to Steve's hip. A soft landing? So far—but he's only half way!

Above centre: Gripping Chris's Judo costume, one hand on the trousers, the other on the collar, Steve begins to straighten and lift. His opponent is forced to come up with him.

Bottom left: Chris is for the mat—hard.

GROUNDHOLDS

On the ground, the action continues. You either get up or get on top. Just as you can lose a match by being thrown to the ground, you can be counted out on the ground.

The idea is to hold your opponent down, their back to the mat. Secure them for thirty seconds and you win, *Ippon*. A lesser time earns a smaller score. Another way of winning is from a submission. This does not mean bending someone's back in two.

Those in trouble, signal. A simple double tapping action with the hand, either on the mat or to the opponent's body, will bring response—immediate release.

Certain moves, recognised as dangerous, are prohibited. Bend the rules and you're penalised. For a serious offence, disqualification.

There are many ways to hold someone down on the ground. You can do this sitting at their side, crouching over or laying across them. As with throws there are standard holds. However, for each of the basic holds there are numerous variations.

Whichever technique you choose the key word is control. The thirty second winning hold-down time will not begin until you have control. Then, of course, you must maintain control. You need to keep the opponent down, their back glued to the floor as they fight on, struggling to escape.

In the following pictures Matthew demonstrates some of the basic holds. He began Judo lessons as a junior player. Now at the age of seventeen he has, since modelling in this book, won his senior brown belt. His opponent here is Paul, who started Judo training in his late twenties.

Left: There is little room for escape from this side four-quarter hold (*Yoko shiho gatame*). Matthew sinks low, his feet, legs spread wide for balance, dig into the mat. This position strengthens the tight grip he has on Paul's belt and collar. Paul finds difficulty in even moving his hips and shoulders—the four quarters of his upper body.

Below: This hold, lengthways four-quarter hold (*Tate shiho gatame*), is very different from other holds. Matthew straddles Paul, pinning him down. It looks a bit of a tangle, and needs a lot of practice—but it works.

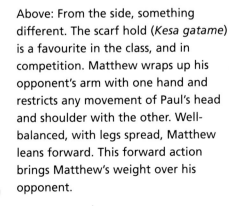

Above: From the side, something different. The scarf hold (*Kesa gatame*) is a favourite in the class, and in competition. Matthew wraps up his opponent's arm with one hand and restricts any movement of Paul's head and shoulder with the other. Well-balanced, with legs spread, Matthew leans forward. This forward action brings Matthew's weight over his opponent.

Matthew approaches from another angle. Both hands grip at his opponent's belt. Now he hauls Paul in. Paul's bracing action, attempting to turn Matthew off, has little effect. This Upper four-quarter hold (*Kami shiho gatame*) is a winner.

The most successful Judo competitor Japan has ever produced is world and Olympic champion Yasuhiro Yamashita, who won the coveted All-Japan Championships nine times. His fighting weight was 127 kilos. In 1985, at the age of twenty-eight, he retired from competition undeafeted. From 1977 until his retirement he achieved 203 successive wins!

Matthew wraps Paul up in a reverse scarf hold (*Kuzure kesa gatame*). Being held down is one thing. Not being able to see what's going on adds to the dilemma!

STRANGLEHOLDS

Strangulation! Not literally. A stranglehold in Judo is not a choke. There is science to the application of these techniques. You must learn how to apply them correctly. Strangleholds pose no danger if rules are followed. You must know how and when to submit if you are under pressure from a stranglehold.

Correct pressure, at the correct point, is the key to a stranglehold. You apply pressure against the arteries of the neck. They carry a supply of blood and oxygen. Cut the supply down and you feel faint. When you feel dizzy on the Judo mat you stop the action. You signal, with a double tapping action of your hand. Immediately your opponent releases their grip. The contest is all over—yes, but you're left fit and ready for another match.

Left: You never squeeze your opponent's neck. That could be dangerous. Tina, in full control, restricts Ruth's head movement to apply the pressure. Ruth submits.

Above: Strangleholds are Tina's forte. Her small hands do not appear threatening. However, she has developed a knack of weaving and twisting them into position for a stranglehold, often unsuspectingly. Her hands, in a scissor-like action, apply pressure to both sides of Ruth's neck. Note how Ruth is about to tap a signal of submission from this cross strangle.

Below right: Tina's right hand takes a grip, high on Ruth's collar, against the far side of the neck. Tina stamps forwards. Her hip acts as a barrier to stop any escape.

Above left: Ruth has been enticed into a trap. As she came forward to make a hold, Tina raised her hips, shooting both legs up around Ruth's head. A triangular stranglehold (*San gaku jime*) is on.

ARMLOCKS

Strangleholds do not mean taking the opponent to the point of death. Armlocks are not applied to cause damage. It is a matter of applying limited pressure.

In Judo you apply pressure to one joint only, the elbow joint. This is done by first restricting the movement of the arm and then putting on the pressure.

Excessive pressure to the joint will cause damage. Most people know of someone who has either broken an arm or a severely torn a ligament.
It must never happen at Judo.

We all know what pain is but we all have different levels of tolerance. You must submit before you feel pain. As soon as your arm feels under strain—tap.

This arm entanglement (*Ude garami*) leaves Paul with one hand free—to tap!

Chris uses his legs to control his opponent's arm. Lifting his hips puts strain on Paul's elbow joint. Paul, of course, submits from this straight arm lock (*Juji gatame*).

GROUND FIGHTING

Groundwork is a safe area for beginners to work in. Equipped with just a few basic skills you can get into the action straight away. You'll soon find how effective, or ineffective the holds can be if you haven't got control.

The most basic techniques of Judo have brought success to world champions. Your stature and strength will determine how you select and refine groundwork moves. Remember though, your opponent will have the same idea as you—to come out on top.

Struggle as he might, Alex can't escape from Luke's hold. These two are training partners—but this time it's for real!

You'll learn how to break through an opponent's defences. Study their weaknesses. Change your grip to confuse and dominate. Attack one way and then another.

Chris's opponent thinks he can bury himself in the mat but there's no hiding in Judo. Chris finds a way in, hooks up and drives off. Thirty seconds later it'll be all over—*Ippon*.

Matthew is sure he won't be caught this time. He keep his arms tucked in. 'No problem' says Chris. He bulldozes forward. At the same time he strips away Matthew's arms—not a text-book hold—but it works!

YOUR FIRST COMPETITION

When you enter in your first competition you'll no doubt be nervous. You'll want to do well and your supporters will be watching. Forget everything else that is going on around you. A word of advice: concentrate on what you're doing. You need all your wits about you. Listen only to the referee. He is there to see fair and safe play. Two corner judges support the referee. They are 'extra pairs of eyes'. Corner judges signal the referee if they see anything happen that they feel the referee may have missed.

Above and left: Judo is full of surprises and ups and downs. Never underestimate your opponent. They may not look like a challenge but give them the slightest chance and it could be all over for you. A good throw is executed with speed, impetus and control— and only takes a couple of seconds. Ask Alex!

Finally, and most importantly. Judo is a sport embodying all that good sportsmanship entails— and more. Go along, you'll find out for yourself.

Part 3
JU-JITSU

Ju-Jitsu is known as 'the art or science of flexibility'. It was one of the first martial arts to be adopted in the West. Its development stems from the many individual arts, some ancient, that either originated in Japan or found their way to Japan from other Asian countries. Just as Ju-Jitsu developed from more ancient arts, many modern martial arts such as Aikido and Judo were born from Ju-Jitsu.

Ju-Jitsu has a vast array of techniques: joint-locking skills, throws, holds, strikes and kicks.

Westerners had never encountered such a complex and effective system of combat skills until the early 1900s, when Ju-Jitsu exponents from Japan travelled abroad. They staged exhibitions, performing extraordinary feats of power and control. So proficient were they at their art that they challenged all comers, including wrestlers and boxers, even two at a time! The results were often brutal, most challengers failing to survive long before submitting or retiring injured.

Today Ju-Jitsu is practised within the safety of organised clubs, each following strict rules of conduct. Techniques are taken only to a point short of threatening damage.

Ju-Jitsu is not a contest of muscular skill or strength. What makes this art so fascinating to both men and women of all heights is its reliance on balance, leverage and speed.

Because of its versatility, Ju-Jitsu is in a continual state of development. It is not surprising that in the modern world a sporting side of Ju-Jitsu flourishes. Kitted out in protective clothing, exponents engage in point scoring bouts. Strict rules specify areas of the body that can be targeted with controlled blows, kicks and strikes. Get in close enough to grapple and you score by throwing your opponent.

Opposite: There are many schools of Ju-Jitsu. Some are traditional in approach and sport plays no part in their study of the art. Some systems emphasise throws and locks others strikes and holds. The possible variations are limitless. It would be foolish to say that one style is right the another wrong. However, one thing is certain—no single system of Ju-Jitsu will ever be called complete.

ANYTHING GOES

If you're already practising a martial art, some of your acquired skills can be put to use in your Ju-Jistu. However, a word of caution: *Proficiency in one art is not a signal to jump into another art feet first.* That would be asking for trouble. Special preparation is needed for the practice of each martial art.

Karate training concentrates on the development of kicking and striking techniques. Breakfall practice, the art of falling without hurting yourself, is not included. On the other hand, the Judo player, an expert in throwing and falling, knows little about punching and striking. A Karate kick, aimed in the middle of a Judo bout, would certainly sound alarm bells!

Whether you're a beginner or an expert in one of the martial arts, tread carefully when you start Ju-Jistu training; take it step by step.

At first, as in Judo practice, you will learn how to fall. Once confident that you can fall safely you'll progress to throwing techniques. Many moves are similar to those in Judo: Remember the sport of Judo was born from the art of Ju-Jistu. The difference in Ju-Jistu is that although in practice there are rules, with safety the major consideration, the application is more brutal. You'll see what I mean.

In real-life situations, faced with an aggressor, you have no time to plan a counter-attack. There are no rules, no boundaries. You need to be able to defend against any attack and, perhaps, even to retaliate.

Ju-Jistu training equips you with an arsenal of defence techniques—throws, locks, strikes, kicks, holds and a lot more. We begin with throws.

Left: Ju-Jistu training deals with reality. An aggressor may spring upon you from behind. You may face an assailant who, before you can respond, grabs hold of you. However alert you are the unexpected happens. You must be prepared for action. Ruth, threatened by Chris, stands no nonsense. Hands and feet at the ready, she speedily reviews her options.

Above: A vigorous palm-heel strike sends her aggressor reeling back—as she intended.

Bottom left and right: With Chris all awash Ruth steps in to finish him off with a major outer reaping throw. Compare this with the same throw in the Judo section where there are rules of play. Same throw—different formula. It's brutal —but it works. This is Ju-Jistu.

Right: In Ju-Jitsu you learn to avoid attack. You either move out of the way or block. You deflect anything that's thrown at you. As Chris comes in to make a grab, Ruth parries his arm. This gives her that vital second to turn the tables.

Above and centre right: Ruth grabs hold, turns in, and throws. It's all over, Chris heads for the mat. In Judo, a sleeve pull lift hip throw—in Ju-Jistu the same. The difference? The start and . . .

Bottom right:
. . . the finish. In a Judo bout Ruth would follow through to the ground to take hold. Here in Ju-Jistu she just follows through with a strike—no nonsense!

Left and right:
Ruth dealt with her aggressor when he either grabbed or attempted to grab her. What about an attacker who comes at you with a punch? Answer: the same, defend and counter. I parry Paul's punching arm and counter-strike.

Now to finish him off. You won't find this throw in your Judo manual!

STAY IN CHARGE

So far Ruth and I, having thrown our attackers to the floor, have chosen to remain standing. We are in charge. Every situation is different and as long as you have the upper hand you can decide what to do next.

We could, as we have demonstrated, follow through with a strike or simply get away. Another way? When you have thrown your assailant to the floor, keep them there. Restrain them. In a Judo contest you hold your opponent down for thirty seconds to score. In Ju-Jistu there are no scores, no clock, no timekeeper. Any restraining technique in Ju-Jistu must put the opponent at your mercy.

A parry with one hand, and a jab with my elbow. This 'opens up' Chris. Now in for the throw.

I'm in control as Chris hits the floor. I stamp forward, my heel aimed at . . .? Entwining my hand around his arm, I bend his elbow joint.

A helping hand ! He's in a painful tangled mess. The pressure's on.

This time, having made the throw, I snap Chris's arm back, elbow against my knee. Such bracing action (if fully applied) could cause severe damage to his joints and ligaments. I'm not finished yet, though.

I wrap his wrist, against the joint, back towards his straining elbow. Now for the lift to make room for me to . . .

. . . settle down. Note: with my calf muscles against his neck on one side, my weight bearing down on the other, I am in position to apply a stranglehold.

TAKE DOWN, KEEP DOWN

So far, in Ju-Jistu practice, we have shown how to ward off an assailant and throw them to the ground. Let's look at another way to floor them; a take-down.

We have shown how, having thrown an attacker to the floor, you maintain control by applying pressure to an an arm joint or by a stranglehold.

You can also apply pressure when they are standing up. Then, in control, you take them to the ground.

Above: I side-step to avoid a punch. My left hand clamps Chris's arm between my neck and shoulder. I whip out with my right arm—a knifehand strike.

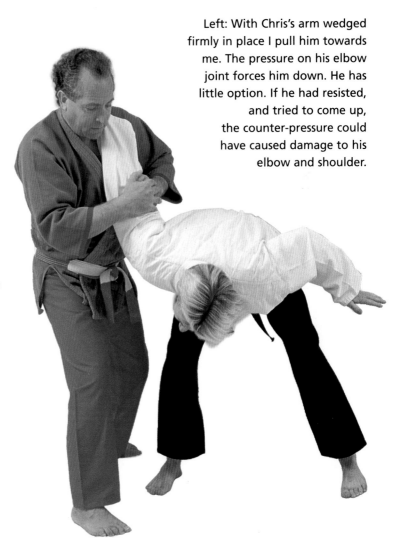

Left: With Chris's arm wedged firmly in place I pull him towards me. The pressure on his elbow joint forces him down. He has little option. If he had resisted, and tried to come up, the counter-pressure could have caused damage to his elbow and shoulder.

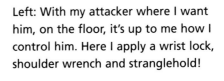

Left: With my attacker where I want him, on the floor, it's up to me how I control him. Here I apply a wrist lock, shoulder wrench and stranglehold!

Above: A one, two action. A parry followed immediately with forearm smash against my attacker's elbow joint. He's on his way down . . .

Left and right: . . . and out. Not literally though. Note: In Ju-Jistu you make full use of your legs. Here my leg keeps Chris's arm twisted and trapped

Left: This double forearm block demonstrates the effectiveness of leverage—two ways—snap! Pulling with my left arm, pushing with my left, quickly sends Chris towards the floor.

Above and bottom left: He hasn't gone all the way. He needs a helping hand, or better still a knee. That does the trick. Chris doesn't think it's at all mysterious—only painful!

FEET FIRST

The initial response to an attack in this section on Ju-Jistu, has been to use the arms to block and parry.

The legs, knees and feet have only come into play to help throw and constrain an aggressor.

The sheer size and weight of a leg makes it a formidable weapon. Now we use the legs and feet as a first line of defence.

Right: Ruth's attacker wants to keep her quiet but soon he'll be the one who's yelling.

Below left and right: A back-heel strike does the job. Chris, distracted and in pain, has no idea what's coming next. Ruth takes advantage of his now relaxed grip on her wrist. She shoots her arm up and grips his wrist. At the same time she turns in towards him. There's her target—his elbow joint

Left and below: A cracking blow takes Chris to the ground where he's trussed up like a turkey.

Left, below and bottom left: This may look like a friendly handshake but Ruth suspects otherwise. Chris's grip is tight. As soon as she feels him pulling she snaps out to strike his shin. It's not enough to knock him down but it gives Ruth time to turn the tables. She controls his arm as she manoeuvres her body.

Right and below: The result: a wrist and shoulder lock that will take him down. Painful? Look at her attacker's face! And for good measure, Ruth, with hand poised, warns him if he even thinks about trying to move.

TWIST AND TURN

Ruth has demonstrated how, by manoeuvring her body, she unbalances and takes control of her attacker.

The way you manage and manoeuvre your body is vital in Ju-Jistu practice. Envision an aggressor entering a department store through revolving doors.

Left, right and bottom left: Block, strike, grip, turn and twist. Note that, having gripped Chris's wrist with both hands, I duck under his arm, turn, and move back. The effect: I've corkscrewed his arm!

Bottom right: Don't forget the breakfall!

If he's allowed to move with the doors' swing he goes happily on. Now suppose you become those revolving doors. You trap him and—smack! You've got him off balance. Now you grip him, move him this way and that, duck, turn and swing, shattering his stability until you have full control. The way you finish him off is up to you.

Ruth demonstrated takedown techniques. Another quick route to the ground—a throw.

Left, bottom left and right:
Another attack. No blocking or striking
needed here just a wrenching twist.

Left: I'm poised ready, as Chris lashes out with a kick.

Above and bottom left: Remember those revolving doors?

AIM AT SURPRISE

A principle of Ju-Jistu practice is 'If it works, do it'. The moves need not be complicated but must be executed with commitment. When faced with danger, get away. If you can use a simple breakaway technique, do so. And remember, the same technique may work in a variety of different situations. A would-be assailant may take you by surprise. By striking back swiftly you can surprise him.

Above and right: Ruth is taken by surprise. And so is Steve!

Left and right: It's full steam ahead, or backwards, in this case.

Bottom right: Steve, winded, tries to regain his balance. Ruth doesn't give him the chance. She reaches back between her legs to . . .

Right and below:
. . . tip him to the mat. A final touch—
she stamps her authority.

STAND AND DELIVER

One way to restrain and control an attacker is to get them to the ground and apply a joint lock or pressure hold. Another way is, while still standing, tie them up in knots.

This method of restraint takes a lot of practice. You must make sure that, having restrained an adversary, you keep the pressure on. There must be no room for retaliation or escape.

Top right and above: Friendly? No. It's time to act and take control. I turn my back on Chris for a split second to deliver an unsuspected blow. Now, to tie him up.

Right: With his arm all askew, straining at the elbow joint, I'm free to bring my other hand into play.

Left: A firm grip needs to be dealt with in a firm way.

Above and bottom left: A quick twist and a turn and Chris knows I mean business. He's on tip-toe stretched to the limit. I'm in complete charge and can march him off.

Left: In this sequence Chris gets wrapped up—with himself! As he makes his strike I side-step and parry. A quick redirection of the offending arm and he'll be mine.

Above and bottom left: Chris is now near to choking on his own actions. Before I grip his belt to lead him away I remind him that I want no further nonsense.

Left: I move in towards my attacker and parry. Dangerous? Yes, for Chris. I follow up immediately with a double strike and . . .

Above and bottom left:
. . . a severe warning. Note: It is best, whenever possible, to move outside and away from an oncoming punch, kick or strike. This action gives you more room and time to make a counter-attack and space to get away. If it's not possible to distance yourself, and you defend by moving towards your attacker, you must do so with lightening speed. You'll be surprised how your reflexes and co-ordination sharpen as you continue to practise Ju-Jistu.

Right: As Paul comes in closer I'm ready for him. I hook one leg behind his ankle and snap out at his knee with the sole and heel of my foot. He's on his way down, I'm on my way up.

DOWN BUT NOT OUT

Consider this—you may be the one on the ground, with your attacker standing. You may have been knocked to the ground. You may simply have been relaxing in a park or on the beach when approached by a would-be assailant.

The idea is to keep the attacker at a distance. Remember, your legs and feet are formidable weapons. It's not always enough to flay them wildly about to ward off an attacker. Make better use of them.

Left: This time Paul approaches from my side. I turn, stop him coming nearer by blocking his front foot with my leg, and smash my other leg into the back of his knee. He collapses forward and . . .

Above:
. . . once he's down I take control. I trap his legs. It's painful. His calf and leg muscles are wrenched against each other. Using my legs to keep him in position, I have him at my fingertips, literally. A slight movement of my hand produces further pressure. It looks brutal, but this is far more than sheer strength. Ju-Jistu is a skill, an art and an activity to enjoy. Whatever you do, safety comes first. However menacing your practice partner may appear, there is never any malice. Now that this session is over, Paul and I enjoy a chat and a drink. Cheers!

Part 4
KARATE

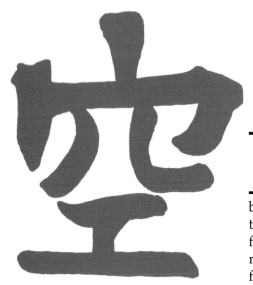

Karate is an art, a sport and a system of physical exercise and defence. It is dynamic yet graceful, subtle yet expansive. Karate was developed and refined in Japan from the fighting arts of Okinawa, an autonomous kingdom between Japan and China up to the later part of the nineteenth century, when it was invaded by Japanese warlords. The new rulers, fearing reprisals, banned the islanders from carrying weapons. In response the Okinawans secretly travelled to China to learn new fighting skills. Soon they had developed a practical system of unarmed combat and formed rebel groups who sprang surprise attacks on their Japanese adversaries.

When Okinawa merged with Japan, the island's martial arts masters were invited to Japan to demonstrate their skills. Gichin Funakoshi was the first to arrive. His display of unarmed combat so impressed the founder of Judo, Jigaro Kano, that he was asked to stay and teach.

Funakoshi, in turn, was inspired by the apparent effect the discipline and etiquette of Kano's system had on Judo students. He introduced a code of conduct into his own teaching and called it Karate, 'The art of empty hands'. The first school he founded, Shotokan, still flourishes to this day and its style is now the most widely practised of all.

With its specific code of behaviour, Karate training continues to be taught because of its benefits to health and self-development. Karate is practised world wide and as an organised sport in European and world Championships.

The following pages show some of the training methods and moves selected from a vast range of skills. As you progress step by step you'll discover the great benefits and enjoyment Karate training can bring you.

THE RIGHT APPROACH

Correct physical preparation for any activity is essential. You also need to be in the right frame of mind. When in the training hall (*dojo*) you switch off from the outside world. You keep your mind on the job in hand.

The idea is to work in safety. Karate, like all martial arts, has rules of play. That's not to say you won't get the odd bump or two along the way. But minimise any unnecessary risk. Stick to the rules; have a clear understanding of what's in store.

The going may get tough at times but you work in an atmosphere of co-operation and friendship.

The class begins in a formal way. Students line up in rows, the teacher out front facing them; it is a time to acknowledge each other's rank and commitment to training. Mutual respect is demonstrated by a simple salutation, a bow, either standing or kneeling. It's now time to discuss any matters concerning training, check everyone is fit to take part, and give instructions for the warm-up period to commence.

Opposite bottom, left and below: Karate training encompasses both power and will-power. Endurance, determination and good spirit will help you win the day. It's not all fight though. Not everyone wants to be a top competitor. Karate training is enjoyed by people of all ages. Start young like this happy bunch and you could be tomorrow's champion.

HAND AND ELBOW STRIKES

When practising Karate you are unarmed. True? In the literal sense yes, but in another sense no. Your body is equipped with 'weapons' to use in defence or attack. Your arms, elbows, hands, legs, knees and feet become the tools of your trade. You'll be taught how to use them in the most effective way, and without causing damage to yourself.

Dave Collacott is a Black belt 4th Dan. He has been practising Karate for more than thirty years. Below, he demonstrates, with one of his pupils, Mark, some of the range of strikes that can be made with the hand and elbow.

Opposite top, and left:
Dave Collacott and his pupil, Mark, demonstrate some of the wide variety of strikes that can be made with the hand and elbow.

Opposite bottom left: This spear hand strike is something quite special. It is an ancient technique used in feudal times by the warriors of Okinawa. They developed the strike by toughening their hands. This was done by severe methods of conditioning. They thrust their fingers repeatedly into jars of pebbles or sand. Their skin toughened and encrusted with large calluses, and their hands became formidably power-ful weapons. Legends are written about these warriors. They could thrust out with a spear hand strike with such power as to pierce through the wood-en armour of an adversary—and deliv-er a fatal blow. Today, these extreme methods of training are not warranted. Such 'toughening' is a potential hazard to health and can lead to arthritis and other joint damage.

KICKING OUT

Dave's son Chris is also a Black belt. Chris is a keen competitor and makes good use of his long legs in competition. The legs, as you know from the section on Taekwondo, can be used effectively in many different ways. Chris knows that to maintain his standard, and his reach, he must never forget the basics. Perfecting posture, position and precision only comes with perseverance and plenty of practice!

STANCE AND STYLE

There are many styles of Karate. Each has its own variations of stance. Some are noticeably deeper or stronger looking than others. Others, almost upright, take on the appearance of a boxer's stance. However, many stances, some with minor modification, are common to all styles of Karate.

An important point common to all styles—it is stressed from the word go that pupils must continue to practise and develop individual stances while practising their kicks and strikes.

Left, bottom left and bottom right: Hayley demonstrates a series of stances. These emphasise a low centre of gravity. Like a tree, the source of strength lies in its roots. From any of these positions Hayley can deliver a powerful kick or blow.

Above and right: There is no one stance to meet all situations. Mark adopts one of the more advanced stances of Karate. Don't be deceived. It may appear more upright than Hayley's, even a little odd. But look closely and you'll note that Mark's hips are lowered—the awareness of an expert ready for anything that is thrown at him.

WHEN TO SWITCH

A stance must never be so rigid that you can't move smoothly to another. That's the next thing to practise. It's also time, moving from one stance to another, to incorporate the punches and kicks you will have learnt. This kind of drill is done with the whole class lined up in rows. The instructor gives a series of commands, one by one, checking to see that everyone has completed the technique correctly before moving on to the next.

The martial arts are for fun and healthy exercise governed by rules that make for safety. There is one activity for arms and legs that has no rules of safety and is designed for injury or worse. It is unarmed combat. This has no interest for us except to acknowledge that it is there and to distance ourselves from it. Unarmed combat is taught in the armed services. It is a killer skill fashioned for life saving in a desperate situation. It concentrates attention on the opponent's most vulnerable points such as heart, throat and kidneys and its aim is total destruction. Unarmed combat is just worth a mention—and then back to happy days with our own martial arts.

Left, right and bottom left: Eleven-year-old Daniel concentrates intently as he glides from one forward stance to another. He has an imaginary opponent in mind and is fully confident of the effectiveness of his movements.

Right: And he lets his ten-year-old sparring partner Jayden know!

Top left, centre and right: From this fighting stance Mark demonstrates perfect control as he makes a front kick (*Mae geri*). An important part of the movement is the knee lift. This allows the leg to move on a shorter axis than if he made a long swinging kick. The result—the leg snaps out with speed.

Bottom: Remember, Karate training involves working both on the right and on the left.

Top left, top centre, top right and opposite: Some Karate moves look deceptively innocent. Who would have thought that the nimble skip Mark makes from his strong straddle stance (*Kiba dachi*) would lead to the delivery of such a powerful thrust kick (*Yoko geri kekomi*)?

The martial arts are not all strong, silent motions of body and limb. Sound plays an important part at times. Judo players are soon familiar with the sharp-sounding crack of the breakfall (the secret of falling safely, slapping the mat with hand and arm). But sound, generated by the body and expelled through the mouth, can also be a formidable weapon. In Karate for instance the kiai, or controlled yell, is developed to a pitch where it startles the opponent, with an almost hypnotic effect. It also generates power in the player who produces it and can have a decisive effect in a contest.

HAND BLOCKING ACTIONS

The blocking actions of Karate, most using arms and hands, need to be performed with care. A hard blocking action, two limbs in direct collision, could inflict pain or damage—upon the defender as well as the attacker. On the battlefield that was all very well. You could say that such an attack and hard blocks are two sides of the same coin.

Today, 'softer' but non-the-less extremely effective blocking methods are used. These, instead of clashing, deflect an oncoming blow. A properly executed blocking action will take you out of immediate danger. At the same time it will weaken the opponent's balance. This puts you in a strong position to counter-attack.

Note how each of Hayley's and Mark's blocking actions are backed with a good stance.

Above: Low sweeping block (*Gedan barai*).

Right: Rising block (*Age uke*).

Left: Outside block (*Soto uke*).

Above: Cross block (*Juji uke*).

BLOCK AND STRIKE

Some training routines can be practised, in safety, away from the *dojo*. Dave and Chris often practise the following kind of sequence together at home. Standing firmly in one spot they don't need a lot of space. Taking it in turns, they block and strike at different target areas of each other's body, high, middle and low.

The action heats up as they throw out the punches with increasing speed. The blocking arm may appear to the untrained eye to crash against the punching arm. This is where the secret skill lies. Look carefully. All the blocks are 'softened' by clever deflecting action, a twisting, rotating motion of the blocking arm on impact.

IT ALL COMES TOGETHER

Now it's all coming together. Stances, blocks, strikes and kicks. We're on the move. And that's exactly what Hayley now needs to do—get moving. To test out her skills under pressure. Who better to put her through her paces than Mark?

Mark knows only too well the effort needed to succeed. This twenty-seven-year old Black belt cheated death seven years ago when he was lying in an intensive care unit after a fire in his home. Smoke inhalation threatened permanent damage to his lungs. However Mark was, and still is, strong-willed and fit. Karate involves stamina training, breathing exercises and a lot more. Mark believes had he not been involved in Karate he would not have survived the ordeal. He has since made a come-back as an international competitor.

The top ranking Karate exponents are Japanese 10th Dans. It takes time! One of these, Hidenori Otsuka, continued practising Karate until shortly before his death—he was 89.

TIME FOR FUN

Let's take a moment off from the rigorous training regime of Karate. We will keep working, but also have fun. There are, of course, many exercises that can be done either solo or with a partner. Sit-ups, press ups, squat thrusts—all rather mundane? Incorporate a little innovation and purpose and they're fun. Take a look at this class: sit-ups—but with a difference. As they come up they alternately strike out at their partner's hand, palm held open.

Right: Jayden enjoys a game of football, but not in the *dojo*. Here, balls are used as a training aid for Karate. As they are thrown from different angles, Jayden must strike out and hit them away. This is a good way to help hone his techniques and sharpen his reflexes.

THE HEART OF KARATE

Kata is the heart of any Karate practice as patterns are in the practice of Taekwondo. Each Kata is performed as a solo exercise.

As a choreographer takes a dancer through a routine, your instructor will take you through a Kata. Step by step, you learn the sequence of moves.

Right: Seven-year-old Christopher intently awaits the next command.

Christopher mirrors the master's every move—a master in the making himself!

Left and right: Having learned the sequence, he's into the swing of it. But that's still not enough. Christopher must master the application of the technique. How does it work?

Bottom left: Ask his opponent, Danny!

DOWN THEY GO

Remember every move in a Kata has a real life application. With so many varied styles there are endless possibilities.

In some Karate classes you use techniques designed to take the opponent to the ground. Just as the Judo expert executes a throw, the Karate practitioner is taught how to topple their partner over. This is often done by making a sweeping action against the legs of the opponent.

Above: As Mark (right) comes in to attack, Chris spins around backwards out of danger. His leg makes a large arc as he ducks and turns in readiness to . . .

Right:
. . . drive back against Mark's leg. Now he can follow up with a strike.

Left: This time Chris defends using one of his neat blocks. As he deflects the oncoming blow he continues to rotate his arm. This enables him to . . .

Below:
. . . grab Mark's sleeve and unbalance him further—with the help of a sweeping action.

Bottom left: Note how instinctively Chris has his right arm poised for action.

ALL UNDER CONTROL

Now it's Mark's turn for action. He's suffered at the hands of other models in this book. Right and below: He challenges Chris.

Right: I told you he was good!

Left: Let's not forget our younger models. They like to spar as well. Jayden (left) tempts Daniel, 'Catch me if you can.'

Above: 'Missed, try again'? It's all in good spirit—it has to be.

Bottom left: Daniel does catch Jayden. It may look a bit underhand, but it's all under control!

Part 5
KUNG FU

功
夫

So far we have dealt with Japanese and Korean martial arts. Now we turn to the Chinese art of Kung Fu. Kung Fu, or Chinese boxing, comes in many hundreds of styles, at least in its external form. The external forms are more obviously physical and referred to as hard styles. The relaxed movements of the internal forms or soft styles, of which there are few, are more concerned with the gathering and sudden release of energy at close quarters.

The harder external Kung Fu systems are said to have originated at a Shaolin monastery where there was a large body of so-called fighting monks. They were not slow to see its value as a self-defence measure if they were waylaid by brigands on their travels. But originally they used Kung Fu for exercise to keep themselves in good trim in the monastery.

Today, people practise Kung Fu for a variety of reasons. However the chief attraction is still the health benefits that training brings.

As for making a choice of style to practise, that shouldn't be too difficult as each system has its own appeal. If you like the look of a particular class, have a go; the odds are you'll enjoy taking part and be hooked.

Right: Lion dancing, which goes back to the Tang dynasty more than a thousand years ago, is still performed in China on special occasions such as the New Year.

ONE STEP AT A TIME

Karate students practise Katas, Taekwondoists perform patterns. Kung Fu students? They also practise movements in prearranged sequences. These are called forms.

Each style of Kung Fu has its own forms. Here, in this section of the book, we take a quick look—for there are an estimated three thousand or more different styles of Kung Fu! Some concentrate on strengthening the legs. This helps develop a strong stance from which kicks and strikes can be executed. Other systems pay particular attention to perfecting close quarter striking and hand techniques.

Whatever style you choose, the major difference between Chinese Kung Fu and Japanese Karate or Korean Taekwondo is that Kung Fu employs very few kicks. These are aimed low. It is rare that a kick is higher than waist level.

When you start to practise Kung Fu, or any other martial art, your actions may appear somewhat robotic. There's nothing wrong with that—it's natural. You first need to learn the sequence, in a clockwork way, step by step. Then, as you become familiar with the form, you find you become more skilled, the moves more refined.

Above: Stephen and Gemma are brother and sister. They practise Tam Toy, one of the external systems of Kung Fu. Their training includes a lot of leg strengthening exercises. That's not surprising—Tam Toy means spring leg. Here, they demonstrate the starting position one of the forms they have been practising for the past year.

Left, below, bottom left and right: As they continue to demonstrate the sequence, note how Stephen and Gemma glide, seemingly effortlessly, from one movement to another. They're good, aren't they?

Opposite bottom: This horse, or straddle stance, is a basic defensive position. The idea, back held straight, is to distribute your body weight evenly between both legs. From here, in perfect balance, you move out of danger or strike out. This position may look easy but it takes practice to get it right. In ancient times students, as part of their training, would have to stand in this position for hours on end. Such arduous methods, which have their dangers, are not used today.

SIMPLE BUT EFFECTIVE

One of the most popular Kung Fu styles world-wide is Wing Chun. It's been practised for some time now—over four hundred years. The originator was a young women, Yim Wing Chun. She studied other Kung Fu systems but found them too complex or reliant on strength. She wanted an uncomplicated yet efficient means of defending herself—for in feudal times there was a real need to equip one's self with self defence skills.

Today Wing Chun remains a practical, no frills,

system. It is combative by nature, but today is practised as an art for enjoyment and self-confidence. It emphasises technique rather than strength and is renowned for subtly shifting footwork and close-quarter hand and arm manoeuvres.

Training includes sparring exercises and the practice of forms. The overall simplicity of Wing Chun is evident by the small number of forms the student has to master—three. None-the-less, mastery of Wing Chun demands full commitment to practice.

Left: For Sarah and Steven, the two students in black at the rear of the class, it's time to learn more moves. They follow the leaders, three Black belt experts who continually strive to improve their own prowess.

Above: From 'Sticking hands' to 'Sticking feet'. This complicates matters. But then life is full of ups and downs.

Opposite below: The challenge—a 'Sticking hand' contest. Mark, (right) and Paul (left) meet in the training hall. They begin with rapid flurries of hand and arm movements and unnerving moments of stillness. Then one breaks through the other's defences. This can take ten minutes or more! When you start to practise you'll get all tangled up. But that's all part of the fun.

KEEP THE UPPER HAND

When you're under attack there is little time to decide what your opponent is doing and how to respond. However, quick action is vital.

If you can anticipate an attack you have a head start. 'Sticking hands', a special Wing Chun exercise, helps here. It is used to develop sensitivity in your hands and arms to the point where it is possible to anticipate the opponent's intentions purely by feel.

'Sticking hands' practice begins with you and your partner standing close to one another. You place you hands, in a guarded way, on their arms. They place their hands similarly on yours. This hands-in-contact keeps you both sensitive to any movement the other makes. As your opponent moves to strike, you follow, hands on, take control and counter-strike—if you can. Don't forget, your opponent is practising too and will try to control your actions.

Above: Meet the two Dereks. Both are Black belts. Derek, on the left, is the teacher (*Sifu*). On the right, Derek his student. Students are naturally eager to pit their skills against their teacher. This doesn't always mean the teacher comes out on top—but they usually do. Here teacher and student practise together. Newly-learnt techniques are being put to the test. As Derek tries out a new hooking movement against his teacher's leg he's in for a surprise.

Bottom right: There's always a move the student hasn't yet found out!

NO-NONSENSE DEFENCE

Many students begin Kung Fu training for self-defence. Its versatility and reliance on technique rather than strength make it appeal to people of all ages and sizes. Kung Fu is quick, sharp and to the point. There are no superfluous techniques.

Above: Meet Sarah. She is married to our Kung Fu instructor, Derek. Sarah wears an Orange sash. That's the level she has reached. Although not as qualified as her Black belt opponent Paul, she certainly knows how to deal with him.

Right: A straightforward no-nonsense parry and strike does the job. This kind of counter-attack combination is common in Wing Chun and many other Kung Fu styles. Remember this—self-defence techniques don't need to have frills, they just need to work.

THE HEALTHY ART

No style of Kung Fu is entirely hard or entirely soft—each contains elements of the other.
Tai chi is the most popular of the softer internal styles of Kung Fu. Most people are attracted to Tai chi for the health benefits practice brings. For many, whose medical conditions prevent them from taking part in other activities, Tai chi is a daily exercise. It can help relieve stress, tone and gently strengthen muscles, aid circulation and heighten awareness.

Most Tai chi students find they feel healthier as

Left, right, opposite top left and right: To the novice, Andrew's graceful, swaying movements, may appear trance-like. Nothing could be further from the fact. He is totally focused. His breathing, perfectly controlled, harmonises with his movements. His mind is relaxed, allowing him to be entirely aware of his surroundings and everything that is going on.

they practise—more vitalised, relaxed and self-confident. For many the combat side of Tai chi is secondary.

Whether you practise for exercise or defence, in Tai chi, like other Kung Fu styles, you practise forms. These solo exercises, sequences of continuous slow-motion rhythmic movements, are central to practice. The movements are designed to allow the body to flow in a relaxed and smooth manner, without interruption, from one stance to another. The idea is to involve the whole body in these actions, at the same time controlling your breathing.

Left, and opposite bottom left and right: Suddenly, but smoothly, without interruption, Andrew moves to a low stance. Then he's back up again, moving on until . . .

Bottom right:
. . . he's finished. And note how relaxed he is. That's the beauty of the art—enjoyment while practising and a sense of wellbeing when you stop to carry on with daily life.

AND IT WORKS

Let's not forget the other side of Tai chi—it's a combat art, self-defence. Because there is little reliance on muscular strength, anyone who is willing to train correctly can enjoy and benefit from practice.

A perquisite to learning martial techniques of Tai chi is the mastery of Tai chi as an exercise. The various defence and fighting applications can only be applied when the movements become second nature. This is true of all martial arts. You first learn the basics: stance, posture, balance, control. Then down to business. But always with care.

Above right: It looks, at first anyway, as if Mark (left) is about to take charge. No chance. Before he knows what's happening he's . . .

Above left: Andrew has parried and captured Mark's arm. Recognise the poise? It's one of the movements from the form he demonstrated. What's next? Well, anything. Andrew's left arm may appear to be doing nothing but wagging a finger at Mark. There's more to it than that. His forearm, firmly in contact with Mark's elbow joint ready to apply pressure, puts Andrew in the driving seat.

Left: . . .out of control! And that's the key to martial arts. Control. You first learn to control your own actions—then you learn to control your opponent's. Now one final word. In practising the martial arts your opponent is your partner. Look after them—and yourself of course. Good luck.

TERMS USED IN THE BOOK

Age uke: Rising block
Dan: Step, Black belt grade
Dojo: Practice hall
Gedan barai: Low sweeping block
Gi: Costume
Ippon: Full point, a win
Juji gatame: Cross straight armlock
Juji uke: Cross block
Kami shiho gatame: Upper four-quarter hold
Kesa gatame: Scarf hold
Kiba dachi: Straddle stance
Kuzure kesa gatame: Broken scarf hold
Mae geri: Front kick
Morote seoinage: Two-handed shoulder throw
Name juji jime: Normal cross strangle
O soto gari: Major outer reaping
San gaku jime: Triangular strangle
Sensei: Teacher
Sode tsurikomi goshi: Sleeve lift, pull, hip throw
Soto uke: Outside block
Ti otoshi: Body drop
Tate shiho gatame: Lengthways four-quarter hold
Tomenage: High circle throw
Uchikomi: Training method, turning in to throw.
Uchi mata: Inner thigh throw
Ude garami: Arm entanglement
Yoko geri kekomi: Thrust kick
Yoko shiho gatame: Side four-quarter hold
Yoko wakare: Side separation throw

ACKNOWLEDGEMENTS

Putting this book together has been much like a stage production. It has involved a large cast who, from audition to opening night (publication), have enthusiastically given their time and expertise.

I cannot name all those involved but would like to say a special thanks and well done to my young models. Their expertise and exuberance gave a lift to the proceedings (sometimes much needed under my direction). They're a credit to their teachers who, waiting in the wings, were seldom needed to prompt in any way.

The teachers I must mention by name: Sensei Dave Collacott 4th Dan, Shotokan Karate; Sensei Martin Hopper 3rd Dan, Taekwondo; Sifu Derek Vernon, Wing Chun and Andrew Thomas, and Tai chi. Their comradeship, generous advice, appreciation and interest in practitioners outside their own ranks epitomise the spirit and underlying philosophy of the martial arts.

Appearing also in the photographs are senior students from the various disciplines. Thanks to you all—a first-class performance.

Included in the senior ranks are a number of students whom I term as part of my extended family. I have watched them grow since they all started their martial arts training with me as young children. My warm thanks to Steven Walter 2nd Dan, Tina Broom 2nd Dan and Chris Ford 2nd Dan. A fourth—my daughter Ruth Goldman 4th Dan. Always on hand, she often bears the brunt of her father's actions—both on and off the mat! Thanks Ruth.

I hope I have not been as fierce towards my loving wife Chris who has supported and bolstered me up over many years. (I am sure, that at times, I must have given more thought and time to the martial arts than might be considered reasonable).

And finally my parents. Mum, although unable now to see the pictures, enjoys and encourages me with my writing. My father, himself an author who inspired me to write, edits my work. His endless appetite for helping me to see my literary efforts in print gives added fervour to my life in the martial arts.

I hope reading this book will encourage you to start practising a martial art. Awaiting is a life-long pleasure.

INDEX